ETCHING AND
DRYPOINT

BY

E. G. PORTER

AUTHOR OF "PRINTING," ETC.

TIDE MILL

Emanuel
Frontispiece

PREFACE

OF the many people who carry out some artistic pursuit as a hobby there are relatively few who have tried etching or drypoint. And this is rather curious because the work is not difficult or expensive; it is fascinating, and has an advantage over drawing and painting, in that the work when done is not confined to a single specimen.

A further advantage that should appeal to those who like variety of occupation is the fact that the work is a combined art and craft; there is first the drawing to be carried out and then the printing to be done, while in etching there is the further interest of biting the plate.

The chief advantage, of course, is that from the artistic point of view an etching or drypoint has a quality and charm quite distinct from any other process. It has a richness and depth of line far removed from that of a pencil drawing, and a texture and variety of line far superior to that of a pen drawing; and, its characteristics once appreciated, a new world of art is opened to the reader, whether he merely admires or also practices.

In its elements either form of art is quite simple, and only requires two talents—patience and the ability to draw. "If you can sketch you can etch," provided there is determination and care; for in spite of the simplicity of the various processes of the work, there is always something liable to go wrong. One great etcher

v

has referred to each work as an "experiment," a statement that, although it may deter some, will merely incite those who look upon everything as an experiment and an outlet for the fighting spirit that is ever eager to combat what seems the inherent obstinacy of the materials we use to express our thoughts and ideas.

Thus, the reader need not despair if his first plate turns out a failure. Many a success is built upon failures, and one plate spoiled will provide many useful lessons. Indeed, even what at first sight seems to be a spoiled plate may be altered and reworked many times until it is brought to a successful issue.

Of the reproductions included in this book some are by schoolboys, and are given not only to illustrate the various processes described in the text, but as examples of what may be done even by children in an elementary school. It is a work that absorbs them, encourages their love of art, and inculcates care and skill and an appreciation of good workmanship. These little works have many defects, which need no apology, as some of them are first attempts, and none of the boys has had more than six months practice in either etching or drypoint.

Of the other plates, the writer has to thank Mr. Frank L. Emanuel for permission to reproduce his two etchings, "Rembrandt at his Press" and "The Tide Mill," and to include the several other plates, Nos. 3, 18, 30, from his "Etching and Etchings," a book that must be read and studied by all who are interested in the art.

Thanks are also due to the British Museum Authorities for permission to copy the eight plates, Nos. 1, 2, 4, 5, 6, 17, 23, 33; while Turner's "Hindhead" is reproduced by kind permission of Messrs. Blackie & Sons from their "Selection from the "Liber Studorium"; and the four plates by E. W. Cooke are taken from his book of "Ships and Shipping," published in 1829.

All these will give the beginner some idea not only of the limitations of the art but of its immense scope. Each art has its own boundaries, and the more a work keeps within those limits the more distinctive it becomes. The essential feature of the etching is its free line, and the best plate technically is the one that insists on this and gets the most value out of it, while the one that tries to become a mezzotint ends in being nothing at all artistically.

But the etched line may be so varied in contour and spacing that it may convey any impression the artist desires; it can express the dark interior of Rembrandt's workshop, or the dazzling daylight of a Tide Mill at Walton on the Naze.

Etching is, we may say, an analytic art. It exhibits the essentials; and it is the faculty for probing into nature and finding its vital outlines that the budding etcher must cultivate.

CONTENTS

PAGE

INTRODUCTION V

CHAPTER I

AN HISTORICAL OUTLINE 1

The beginnings of etching and drypoint—Great etchers and their work

CHAPTER II

ETCHING AND DRYPOINT 11

Outline of processes—Their differences in technique and appearance—Preparing the drawing

CHAPTER III

DRYPOINT 19

Detailed discussion—Work with compressed fibre—Preparing and printing—Drypoint on metal

CHAPTER IV

ETCHING 29

Preparation of plate — Grounding — Needling — Etching — Stopping out — Reworking — Aquatint —Soft ground etching

CHAPTER V

PRINTING 63

The press—Paper—Ink—Faults in printing—After treatments of proofs—Mounting

CHAPTER VI

PAGE

HOME-MADE APPARATUS AND MATERIALS .   . 76

Plates—Grounds—Dabber—Hot plate and jigger—
Mordants and stopping-out varnish—Burnisher—
Scraper—Wooden press—Preserving plates.

APPENDIX 89

Recipes—Abbreviations—Materials required

ILLUSTRATIONS

PLATE   PAGE

Tide Mill. *Emanuel* . . . . *Frontispiece*

1. The Prodigal Son. *Dürer* 2
2. Bear Hunt. *Hirschvogel* 4
3. The Market Horse. *Gerard* 6
4. The Drummer. *Callot* 7
5. The Three Trees. *Rembrandt* 8
6. Perseus Killing Medusa. *A. Runciman* . . . 9
7. Hindhead. *Turner* 12
8. Lines made by Etching and Drypoint (diagram) . 14
9. A Footballer (drypoint on fibre) 16
10. Narcissus (drypoint on fibre) 17
11. Drypoint Knife and Holder (diagram) . . . 20
12. Lines Cut on Fibre 22
13. Cottage (drypoint on fibre) 23
14. Crocuses (drypoint on fibre) 25
15. A Boat (drypoint on fibre) 26
16. A Church (drypoint on zinc) 27
17. Cottage by Water. *Rembrandt* 30
18. Sheep in Shade. *J. Linnell* 32
19. Fishing Boat. *Cooke* 34
20. Rembrandt at his Press. *Emanuel* . . . 37
21. Dutch Galliot. *Cooke* 39
22. Experimental Plate (etching) 42
23. Man with Spade. *Callot* 43
24 (*a*) and (*b*). Bridge (two states) 46
25. Boat with Sky 47
26. Wooden Bridge 48
27. Fishing Boat Arrived. *Cooke* 50
28. Yarmouth Herring Boat. *Cooke* 52
29. Test Plate (aquatint) 54
30. Firs. *J. Cozens* 56
31. Trees (soft ground) 57

PLATE   PAGE
32. Boat (soft ground)   59
33. Old Man Gazing at Tombstone. *Gainsborough* .   . 61
34. Copper-plate Press (block)   64
35 (*a*) and (*b*). Barn (two proofs) 66
36. Cottage   68
37. A Mount—to Cut (diagram) 72
38. A Mounted Etching (diagram)   74
39. A Dabber   77
40. Hot Plate and Jigger   79
41. Burnisher and Scraper 81
42. Photograph of Wooden Press   83
43. Iron Plate for Wooden Press 85

ETCHING AND DRYPOINT

CHAPTER I

AN HISTORICAL OUTLINE

THERE are three methods of printing, as the design which is inked, and thus reproduced on paper, may be either raised, sunk, or on the surface of the material used.

The first is the method of wood and line blocks and of printing type, and the last is known as lithography from the stone which was always used for this purpose, although now much of the work is done on metal plates.

It is with the second method that this book deals, a process known as Intaglio printing (from the Italian *intaglio*, to cut in), this word being first used to denote any figure or design, as in jewellery, cut below the surface as opposed to *cameo*, which has the figures in relief. It is thus in essence a very old art, as the seals of ancient times were intaglios and the wax impressions the "prints." Drypoint goes back even to prehistoric times, for although the sketches of the cave men on rocks and bone were never printed, yet they were done in a way similar to the modern drypoint plate.

Printing, however, is a fairly modern art, made possible by the introduction of paper into Europe in

PLATE 1

THE PRODIGAL SON   *Dürer*

the Middle Ages, and when we now speak of an engraving, etching or drypoint, we refer to the prints obtained by these processes and not to the plates prepared by the artist. His whole aim in working on the metal is to produce a work of art on paper, and when he has printed an "edition" of some dozens of proofs the plate is destroyed.

Intaglio printing now has various forms, such as engraving, drypoint, etching, aquatint and mezzotint, and as with so many discoveries in both science and art, the beginnings of etching and drypoint (with which we are here chiefly concerned) have no historic detail.

The word *etch* is derived from the Old High German *ezjan*, "to cause to eat" (the German being aetzen "to bite or corrode," as with an acid) and both in Germany and Holland the art of biting metal plates with acid was first practiced at the beginning of the sixteenth century. It developed from the work of the armourers and jewellers of the previous century; those fine artists who engraved (or cut) intricate patterns on weapons and ornaments. In order to test the progress of their work they used to fill in the incised lines with some sort of black paste or paint. This made the engraved portions stand out boldly, and an even clearer view of the work could be obtained by pressing on to the metal thus treated a piece of paper, so that it would pick up the coloured matter and so provide a print of it. These prints were indeed often preserved as records of the work done.

It was no far step from this for artists to engrave designs or pictures on flat metal plates in order to obtain prints in a like manner, and as the earlier metal workers had also called in the aid of acid to eat out

BEAR HUNT PLATE 2 *Hirschvogel*

their designs, so the artists also began to use this method and *etch* their plates.

Thus, the first known intaglio prints are *engravings*—these being done with a burin or graver, a wedge shaped tool which was pushed through the metal; an art which reached its fullest development in the hands of Dürer (1471–1528) and declined into mere mechanical work in the last century. At the time of Dürer there also developed very rapidly the method of drypoint in which the metal was scratched with a sharp steel point held like the pencil, and not pushed through the metal like the graver. The earliest works we have of this kind are by an unknown artist—the Master of the Hausbuch* who worked about 1480, but Dürer himself did three drypoints in 1512.

The practice of etching the plate also developed at that time, the earliest dated work from a plate bitten by acid being by Urs Graf in 1513, although Daniel Hopfer probably produced some of his etchings before this as he is entered on the register of a guild of Augsburg as an engraver of copper in 1500.

Dürer etched six plates in the period, 1515–1518, and Hirschvogel, who lived in the first half of the sixteenth century, saw the advantage of various strengths of line, and probably obtained them by using needles of varying thickness rather than by the more modern method of biting for various times in order to etch the lines different depths. A work of this period by M. Gerard (Plate 3) while showing delightfully delicate needling

* The names of some of the earliest artists are unknown, and they are, therefore, called by some sign they used, as the "Master of the Crayfish," or by some work they produced, as in the above case; although it is doubtful whether the "Hausbuch" was entirely the work of this master.

and biting, lacks aerial perspective owing to this lack of contrast.

The French artist, J. Callot (1592–1635) produced a very large number of etchings and became very popular, and his work had some influence on succeeding artists, such as Claude (1600–1682) and even Rembrandt (1606–1669). A very great etcher of this period was Van Dyck

PLATE 3

THE MARKET HORSE   *Gerard*

(1599–1641) "the solitary great etcher" of the Rubens school, although he only produced twenty-one plates; but the greatest of all was (and is) Rembrandt. His work shows immense variety of style and he exploited every known means for obtaining effect.

The first great etchers of Great Britain were the brothers Runciman—Alexander (1736–1785) and John (1744–1768), but in the eighteenth and nineteenth centuries most of the great painters also worked on metal. John Chrome, Gainsborough, and Turner produced soft ground etchings, but the greatest work of the latter consisted of etchings for the Liber Studiorum.

PLATE 4

THE DRUMMER   *Callot*

(original size)

(Note the immense number of active figures in the vivid little etching)

A hundred plates were projected for this collection of landscapes, "Historical, Mountainous, Pastoral, Marine and Architectural," but not all were published. Turner etched the plates in outline and left the work to be finished as mezzotints by others in accordance with his detailed instructions. The beauty of his plates and the immense amount he could convey by mere outlines will be seen by a careful study of Plate 7.

THE THREE TREES

PLATE 5

Rembrandt

PLATE 6

PERSEUS KILLING MEDUSA

A. Runciman

Of other artists that must be mentioned, there is
Goya (1746–1828) of Saragossa, whose aquatints are of
superlative worth, and Meryon (1821–1868) of Paris,
whose etchings, especially of architecture, have greatly
influenced modern artists. The etchings of W. Cooke,
at the beginning of the nineteenth century, being
chiefly devoted to shipping, are interesting for their
delicate work and accuracy of detail.

Haden and Whistler were among the finest etchers
at the close of the last century, and to-day there are
so many artists of outstanding merit that it would be
invidious to mention but a few. The very full list of
past and present masters included in "Etching and
Etchings" will be found most useful for reference, and
the beginner in this art should study all the prints he
can in museums and art galleries, and in good books of
reproductions.

CHAPTER II

ETCHING AND DRYPOINT

OWING to the many points of similarity in Etching and Drypoint they are often confused and their remarkable differences not generally understood. It is true that in each case grooves are made in the metal, and that these are filled with ink and printed from, but the methods of making these incisions constitute two different arts.

In etching the plate is covered with an acid-resisting medium and the artist uses a needle somewhat in the manner of a pencil to scratch through this very thin surface. If the plate has been properly prepared and the etching needle suitably pointed the latter moves quite freely over the surface of the plate, and only enough pressure is required to make the surface of the metal clean and bright. It is not necessary to scratch the plate, and indeed so doing may lead to unfortunate results. Neither is it necessary to attempt varying thicknesses of line, for this work is done with the acid and not with the needle at all.

Thus, in etching, the needle is easily under control as it practically slides over the plate, and a large amount of the work is done in the acid bath, in which process the plate is carefully watched. When the lightest lines of the picture are considered to be etched deep enough the plate is removed from the acid and dried, and those lines covered with an acid resistant so that they shall not be further bitten. The plate is then re-immersed and the next deeper lines watched and stopped at the

11

PLATE 7

HINDHEAD

J. M. W. Turner

right moment; and so on until the darkest portions of the picture—which have been etching during the whole of the period—are thought to be satisfactory.

Then when the plate is inked the lines of varying depths hold proportional quantities of ink, and the proof shows several qualities of line.

With Drypoint, on the other hand, as its name implies, no acid is used and the plate is worked upon in its polished state. It has not to be covered with any medium nor is it immersed in any mordant. The required lines are merely scratched upon it with a sharp and hard steel needle, or a diamond called (rather confusingly) a drypoint. The word drypoint is thus used to denote both the print and the tool with which the plate is scratched.

In this process the needle has to be pressed into the plate and, naturally, this effort retards the freedom of the hand. The pressure is regulated according to the depth of line required, and the needle is held generally on the slant, so that as it cuts into the plate it throws up a burr on one side of the line. This burr is of value in holding the ink and gives a richness of effect that is one of the qualities of a drypoint. All the work is done with the needle, and when finished the plate is printed in a similar manner to the etching.

That is to say, ink is pressed firmly into the incisions, the surface of the plate is wiped clean, covered with a printing paper, and passed through the press. A difference in the lines produced by the two processes depends on the way the ink is held by the metal, Plate 8 illustrating (C and D) the line in an etched plate made by the acid, and (A) the drypoint line which is widest at the surface, and has a ridge or burr at one side.

It will thus be seen that whereas drypoint consists of
one process, etching consists of two equally important
ones. In the former method the power of the line
is controlled by the needle, and in the latter by the
acid; and while the mobility of the etching needle is a
great advantage, yet the management of the actual
etching in the bath, although it gives an added control,

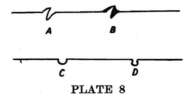

PLATE 8

A. Line cut by drypoint.
B. Line cut with ink.
C. Line cut by quick mordant.
D. Line cut by slow mordant.

may be—especially in the hands of the inexperienced—
a rather hazardous experiment.

The two methods are often combined, the artist
outlining his etching in drypoint, or strengthening some
of the lines in this way. In this case the burr of the
drypoint may be removed with a scraper.*

In any case the burr will not survive many impressions, for the pressure required to force the paper into
the lines in order to pick up the ink is so great that the
burr is soon worn off, and a drypoint plate will only
produce about a quarter of the number of prints that
an etched plate will. In order to strengthen the surface
in either process many artists have their plates steel

* Many of the earlier masters made use of the burin also and
thus combined etching and engraving. This may be noted especially
in the works of Hirschvogel and Callot, while Dürer's works on metal
were practically all engravings.

faced by electrolysis, but, of course, the amateur will not need to do this. Only a dozen or so proofs will generally be required, and a drypoint, even on compressed fibre (to be dealt with in a later chapter) will supply these, while fifty or more etchings may be obtained from a zinc plate.

The difference between etching and drypoint having been made plain, it is obvious that the artist should start with a clear idea of what he means to produce so that he may use the process most suitable and convenient for that end. If the picture is to contain a mass of lines the smooth-running etching needle will be found most easy to manipulate, but if bold simple outlines are desired the drypoint may be the best medium. But each worker really suits himself, and once he has mastered either medium adapts it to his own requirements. The chief drawback in drypoint is that the plate soon wears down, while to the beginner the fact that the needle is not free-running is its chief disadvantage. The proper plan is to give both arts a good trial and use either as occasion demands or experience dictates.

PREPARING THE DRAWING. The best way of going to work is to make a careful pen drawing of the desired picture, the actual size of the plate to be used : whether the work be original or a copy this is by far the best plan. Draw with the idea of etching or drypoint (whichever is decided upon for this particular study) constantly in mind.

From this drawing a tracing can be made—not necessarily of all the detail—but of the general outlines, and this tracing transferred to the plate by means of carbon paper so that there will be no fumbling when

PLATE 9

A FOOTBALLER   J. Rogers (age 13)

the real work commences. It is here that a slight difficulty will present itself, for by contact printing everything is reversed. If we wish the print exactly like the preliminary drawing, the tracing must be

PLATE 10

NARCISSUS   *W. Laskey (age* 11)

reversed and the needling worked in reverse; if this is not done the finished print will be a "looking-glass" one.

In the first case the difficulty will be in the needling, and in the latter case in the comparison of proof and drawing, and in subsequent working. The use of a small mirror, in which either drawing or print may be viewed, will obviate either difficulty, and, as the first working on the plate is by far the bigger operation, this is generally done the right way round, even by great artists, many of whose etchings will show left-handed people, well-known buildings in reverse, and even backward lettering. When the artist works his plate in the open, sketching direct from nature, this method is, of course, inevitable.

Having thus got the drawing on to the plate it is essential that the work be carried on with great care, for alterations form the most laborious part of the whole process. It is one thing to add fresh detail (and as we shall see, it is often advisable to work the picture in sections), but it is quite another matter to alter or erase any lines once they are made. The artist will indeed rework his plate many times so that the time already spent shall not be wasted or the original idea lost—as it may be if the picture is restarted; but the beginner will probably do better to start afresh if the work has somehow or other got out of hand.

SIZES OF PLATES. Before considering the processes in detail, a few words are advisable on the sizes of plates to be used. With the average amateur the question of cost is often an important consideration, and if only for this reason it would be best to commence in a small way. Good zinc plate costs at least a farthing a square inch, and the copper-plate press to print a plate over five inches wide will cost more than £4.

Working on a small scale will thus be economical, and it will encourage a love for small delicate work and the power to express much in a small space.

CHAPTER III

As explained in the previous chapter, a drypoint is worked on a clean plate with a very hard and sharp needle of steel, or a precious stone (diamond, ruby, sapphire) set in a holder so that it cuts somewhat like the glazier's diamond. This point not only cuts to various depths according to the pressure used, but throws up a burr of varying degree according to the angle at which it is held. Used on the slant, like a pen, it throws up a burr on one side, but if held upright the burr is formed on both sides of the line. The ink is held both by the groove and the burr, as shown in Plate 8 (*B*), and thus gives a different impression from the simple furrow of the etched line.

The beginner will find the drypoint more difficult to use than the etching needle, because the hand cannot move so freely, and it is difficult to judge the effect each line will produce in the proof. There is, however, a process on the market which is very suitable for the amateur, consisting as it does of scoring a compressed sheet of fibre with a knife or needle. It is this form of drypoint which we shall describe here, leaving it for the more ambitious who wish to work with metal to experiment on practically the same lines, or to consult more advanced textbooks on the subject.

DRYPOINT ON FIBRE. The compressed fibre is practically a thin cardboard treated so that it has a hard texture throughout and a glossy surface, from which

19

all ink may be wiped. It can be purchased quite cheaply, and although it will not yield anything like the number of prints that a metal plate will do, it will yet produce delightful results.

It is somewhat similar to the compressed fibre of which attaché cases are made, and if the reader can obtain any such material (with a smooth surface) it will serve an excellent purpose for practice. Some of

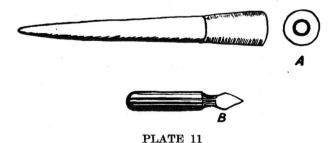

PLATE 11

A PENHOLDER (WITH END AS *A*) SUITABLE FOR USE WITH DRYPOINT KNIFE *B*

the illustrations for this chapter have been done on odd scraps of such material obtained by the boys from an adjacent factory.

THE DRYPOINT. The best tool to use is an arrow pointed knife (Plate 11 *B*), and these may be obtained like pen nibs and fitted into a pen holder, which should be a fairly heavy wooden one with a circular slot, (*A*), at the end for holding the nib (Plate 11).

The holder is then used in much the same way as a pen, cutting into the card lightly or heavily, as required. It will be found necessary to turn the card round at various angles in order to work the various lines and curves, as it must be remembered that each cut with the knife should throw up a burr: it is not sufficient just to scratch the card. Some practice should be made on a spare piece of material in order to obtain a mastery of the implement, with various forms of lines and varying pressures. A proof taken from this will show what effects such work really produces (Plate 12).

Having decided upon the sketch to be reproduced— something simple to begin with—and prepared the drawing in ink, a piece of card is cut to the required size. This must be done with a sharp knife, and a fairly heavy one, for the card is very hard. If the edge is burred by the knife it must be rubbed smooth with a paper knife or some such object or it will print as a heavy black line.

TRACING. Now a tracing of the drawing may be taken and transferred to the plate (as we may as well call the card) by means of carbon paper. It is only necessary to trace the chief outlines, and when transferring it to the plate do not press hard enough to indent it or such marks will afterwards print.

When the outlines are on the plate, and they will be most clearly visible in a strong *side* light, the work with the knife may be commenced, using it as found most suitable by the preliminary practice, and working outlines and shading together from the prepared drawing.

Use the tool as easily and lightly as possible, bearing in mind that lines may be strengthened afterwards, although it will be difficult to weaken them, and impossible to erase them. The worker on a metal plate may scratch the metal away where there is an unwanted line, and then repolish the surface at that

3—(734)

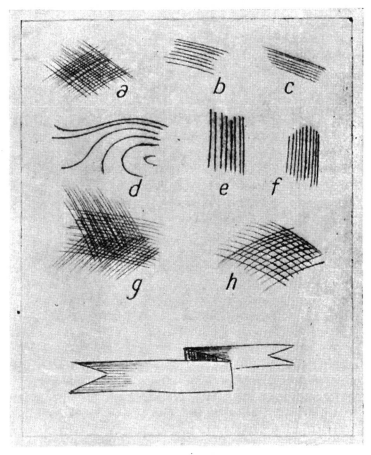

PLATE 12

LINES, CUT IN COMPRESSED FIBRE, OF VARIOUS
STRENGTH AND DIRECTION

spot, but, of course, this remedy is impracticable with card.

TESTING. In order to test the work as it proceeds it will be found a good plan to blacken the lines every now and then. To do this take a very little powdered blacklead on a piece of rag and wipe it over the plate;

PLATE 13

A COTTAGE   J. Rogers (age 13)

the powder will then fill the lines while the smooth parts of the plate will wipe quite clean.

When the plate is considered finished a trial proof is taken and compared with the original. Then lines that require strengthening may be reworked, further details may be inserted if desired, and faulty lines may, perhaps, be worked over into shadow.

PRINTING. Printing will be discussed fully in a later chapter, but it had better be pointed out here that when using this compressed fibre a slightly different method of inking and printing must be used from that employed with metal plates. The ink must be fairly thin (for heat cannot be employed in this process) and the pressure of the rollers must not be too great or the drypoint lines will be badly injured or even destroyed.

INK. Thus, the best material for this purpose is printer's ink, which may be taken up on an inking pad and wiped over the plate, working it into the incisions. This ink will be found firm enough to hold in the lines when the plate is wiped clean with a piece of rag; a process that may be facilitated in very cold weather by holding the plate near the fire (but not too near) for a few seconds.

PRESSURE. When passing the inked plate through the press make certain that the pressure will not be too great by adjusting the blankets beforehand and running them through the rollers with a piece of waste fibre. By getting just the right degree of pressure a good many prints may be obtained before there is any decided falling off in the quality of the lines, and it is, therefore, imperative to be careful in this matter. If the pressure is too light at the first pull, it may be increased by degrees until just right, without any wear to the plate, but if too great in the first instance much work will be lost that can never be regained.

The illustrations to this chapter show what may be done by this process even in a simple way, being copied by boys from Littlejohn's "Art for All" drawing books. As will be seen, some difficulty was experienced with curved lines, especially of a formal nature such as

PLATE 14

CROCUSES   *J. Bastick (age 11)*

the bowl in Plate 14. The lightness of Plate 13 is due
to lack of pressure on the knife, which in Plate 14 was
used rather too heavily for the subject. Plate 36
shows some delicate shading enhanced by retroussage.

PLATE 15

A Boat   *E. Agass (age 13)*

DRYPOINT ON METAL. If the reader is tempted to
go further with this work and use metal plates, the
only requirements are smooth zinc of a thickness that
will not easily bend, and a hard steel pointed tool.

PLATE 16

A First Attempt at Drypoint   *E. Agass (age* 13)
ON A ZINC PLATE

Plate 16 shows a first attempt at this work, on a piece of zinc (18 S.G.) cleaned with metal polish. The tool was merely a dart with a heavy handle, the end kept to a keen cutting point by frequent sharpening on an oil stone. A little preliminary sketching on an old piece of zinc will soon show how best to use the drypoint, and feeling the burr on the smooth zinc with the finger tip will show if the point is cutting properly.

A drypoint on metal should be printed in an exactly similar manner to the etchings as described in Chapter V, using copper-plate ink and the heater, etc.

It will be noted that heavy shadows (such as the porch in Plate 16) come out much better in a drypoint than in an etching. If the lines are placed very close together in an etching and then bitten deeply, they will foul and break, leaving places that will not hold the ink. In a drypoint there is no fear of this, and as both groove and burr hold the ink, the lines, if very near one another, will not print separately, for it will be impossible to wipe clean the minute spaces between them. This is a point that must be borne in mind when working. If clean lines are wanted they must be fairly widely spaced, or worked very lightly, or the burr must be taken off with the scraper.

A convenient method of tracing the picture on to the smooth metal is to rub the back of the tracing paper, on which the drawing has been made, with a stick of damp chalk. Then lay it on the plate with this chalked surface against the zinc and go over the outlines with a hard pencil. The picture will then appear in white lines clearly visible on the plate.

CHAPTER IV

ETCHING

THERE are several metals suitable for etching, each having its advantages and disadvantages. The metal must be hard enough to withstand the strain of the printing press, but soft enough to polish to a high degree with little labour; it must be pervious to some common acid and of a close grain or texture so that minute portions left standing between etched lines will not break down under the roller of the press.

It must also, of course, be fairly cheap, and to-day the two metals that satisfy these requirements in a most satisfactory manner are copper and zinc. The latter is the more liable to break down and so deteriorate more quickly during the printing, but neither will give more than about a hundred prints, the quantity depending on the quality of the etching. A plate with large clear areas and lines wide apart will allow of many more proofs than one with close networks of lines, although even so the edges of the lines begin to wear away, and the broad polished spaces seem somehow or other to become less clear and marked with scratches. As the working of both metals is similar, the instructions which follow, although confined to zinc, will serve for, either, the chief difference being that copper requires a stronger mordant than zinc.

THE PLATE. The first necessity in etching is naturally the plate, which may be purchased in varying grades of finish. It is best obtained polished and cut to size, although large plates may be got and cut as wanted, or plates may be had cut, bevelled and grounded by the manufacturer.

For practice work ordinary sheet zinc may be prepared, as explained in the next chapter, but for good

PLATE 17

COTTAGE BY WATER　　　　　　　　　　　　*Rembrandt*

work it is necessary to purchase properly-prepared plates, the cheapest method being to order a pound or two of odd sizes. They will be from two or three inches square to rectangular pieces about four by six inches, sizes quite large enough for any amount of good work.

Having decided upon the work to be etched, and prepared a sketch (preferably in pen and ink), a plate of suitable size is selected, great care being taken to preserve its polish and keep it free from even minute scratches. If it is a little larger than the picture the surrounding border must be kept free from blemish unless it is to be cut off afterwards, as the whole of the plate is printed and leaves an indented margin (called the plate mark) round the edges which must be preserved.

SMOOTHING AND BEVELLING THE EDGES. Because of this plate mark it is necessary to smooth the edges of the zinc, this being done with a fine file, and finished with a burnisher. The edge of the polished surface is then slightly bevelled—about one third down the side— and polished, for a sharp edge will cut the paper and the blanket, destroying the value of the print and injuring the blanketing. When filing be particularly careful to see that none of the filings rest on the surface of the plate or they will scratch it; keep the plate dusted with a soft brush, such as an old shaving brush.

This process of finishing off the edges is often left until the etching is completed. One advantage of this is that if the plate is spoiled it will not have to be done at all, and another is that the ground on the edges will probably get scratched in the processes of needling and etching, and will become roughened by the acid in the bath, which will necessitate repolishing. In either case it is necessary to see that the edges are bevelled and polished before printing, for a cut blanket is useless, and unless the polishing is well done, the edges will hold the ink and the plate mark will be dark and patchy instead of being clean.

GROUNDING THE PLATE. The polished surface is then covered with a thin film of acid-resisting material called a ground. This must have three qualities—it must go on evenly, it must remain on where necessary

SHEEP IN SHADE

PLATE 18

J. Linne

while under the attack of the acid, and it must be
easily penetrated by the etching needle without flaking
or chipping in any way.

Before apply the ground the plate must be thoroughly cleaned from grease, which may be done by
wiping it with a clean rag dipped in turpentine or
methylated spirit. On no account let the fingers come
in contact with the surface after this is done. The plate
must be manipulated by gripping two opposite edges
between finger and thumb, just as the photographer
handles his plates.

LIQUID GROUND. If a liquid ground is obtained it
is applied thus. The plate is held on the slant over
a dish (polished side uppermost) and the liquid poured
along the top edge so that it runs down and covers
the plate, which is then stood on edge to dry, leaning
against some object with the ground on the underside
so that no dust will settle on it. The liquid must then
be poured back into the bottle through a funnel in
which a small cotton wad has been placed to filter off
any specks of solid matter, for such will render the
liquid useless, and all this must be done quickly, for the
liquid in which the ground has been dissolved evapor-
ates very rapidly and the solution will soon become too
thick for use.

SOLID GROUND. This is obtained in a ball and is
applied to a heated plate. A black ground is most
suitable as it will show up most clearly the lines as they
are needled. For this method (and also for inking) a
hot plate and a jigger are required. The former is
heated by a gas burner or a spirit lamp, and the latter
is merely a box placed on its side. They are placed
together on the table as in Plate 40, so that the zinc

plate may be slid from one to the other. For large
plates it will be necessary to have a small hand-vice,
which grips the corner of the plate when too hot to

PLATE 19

FISHING BOAT   E. W. Cooke

handle, but this can be dispensed with when using small
plates, as they can be shifted along with a paper knife or
some such object if the two platforms are exactly level,
and care is taken not to touch the surface of the zinc.

Keep the burner under one end of the hot plate so that there will be varying degrees of heat thereon, and place the zinc on top to become warm. Then take the ball of ground and rub it lightly upon it with a curving or zigzag motion, and if the zinc is hot enough the ground will melt. Do not apply too much. Now slide the plate on to the jigger, and while it is still hot make the ground even with a dabber—a small pad of silk or chamois leather stuffed with rag. Use the dabber first with a rolling motion in order to spread the ground evenly, and then use a light dabbing motion, which will give a kind of stippled effect over the whole plate. If the ground gets sticky the plate has become too cold and must be reheated, but if the work is done quickly the ground will spread very evenly and thinly over the whole surface. When this is accomplished slide the plate back to the heater and in a few seconds the ground will become glossy again. Directly this occurs it is shifted back to the jigger to get cold. If too much heat is applied the ground will begin to bubble and will be spoiled, and if it is burned in any portion the plate must be cleaned with turps and reground.

The chief mistake made in laying the ground is to make it too thick. It is astonishing what a thin layer is really necessary and the reader should try grounding a few plates, and then cleaning them again, if necessary, until he can obtain a very thin and even film all over the plate. It is obvious that the thinner the ground the easier and more reliable the needling will be, so that this matter is worth a little preliminary practice.

SMOKING THE PLATE. It is usual, but not necessary, to smoke the ground before going any farther. This will enable a clearer tracing to be made on it, and also show up the needling more clearly. It is done by holding the plate face downwards in the hand-vice in one hand, while the other hand moves a small bundle of lighted tapers below it so that the sooty smoke collects evenly on the ground without burning it. The plate is then placed on the heater until the ground shines once more. This incorporates the soot with the ground so that it will not rub off when handled. As before, if any part is burned the plate must be cleaned and reground.

As we have said, this process is not really necessary, and the tracing may be made straight onto the ground. For this purpose a light-coloured transfer paper is placed between the tracing and the plate, and the main outlines gone over with a hard pencil. The lines on the plate will not be very clear, but will show sufficiently to work from in a side light.

NEEDLING. Do not go over the lines laboriously, but sketch with the needle as freely and lightly as possible. The needle must, of course, penetrate the ground, scraping it off in fine shavings and thus exposing the shining white surface of the zinc. But needless pressure, besides destroying the freedom of the sketching, will scratch the metal and give a bigger area for the acid to attack in the bath. Thus, uneven needling will cause uneven biting, and any wrong line done with enough pressure to scratch the plate will print as a drypoint line. If, however, the needle only moves over the surface of the plate, any unwanted line may be stopped out before the etching is done and thus got rid of completely.

Having done the outlines as traced on the ground, all the shading and details may be put in from the sketch. Remember that lines may be bitten to different

PLATE 20

REMBRANDT AT HIS PRESS   *Emanuel*

depths, so that those which will be etched longest must be farthest apart, for if they are too close together the metal left standing between them will be too weakened and will break down in the printing. Hence, the general rule is :—distance—light lines close together; foreground—heavy lines wide apart : heavy and light referring, of course, not to the needling, but to the etching process, and close and wide being relative terms indicating (in the best work) thousandths of an inch.

The reader may purchase a specially manufactured needle for this work, or he may use—just a needle. Any needle will do, from a sewing needle to a gramophone needle, but it must be thick enough not to bend in use, and mounted firmly in a wooden holder that will be comfortable to the hand in sketching. It must not be too sharp or it will catch in the metal, and the best way to give it a nice smooth flowing point is to draw with it on a piece of cardboard a spiral line, commencing with a big sweep and gradually getting smaller and smaller, and holding the needle more upright. This, without spoiling the point, will give it a smooth rounded end, and as this will wear off with use the needle must be sharpened on a stone or a new needle substituted and smoothed.

PAINTING BACK AND EDGES. When the needling is finished the edges and back of the plate must be covered with an acid-resistant. This may consist of shellac varnish, stove enamel, brunswick black, or any such material, put on with a brush so that no part of the metal (except that needled) is left bare. When this is dry the plate is ready for the next stage.

Etching consists merely in placing the metal in a

PLATE 21

DUTCH GALLIOT, ETC. (UNLOADING).   *E. W. Cooke*
GT. YARMOUTH

bath of *mordant*; that is, some liquid which will dissolve the metal. Nitric or hydrochloric acid or perchloride of iron is generally used, and the bath is just a shallow dish such as photographers use.

THE MORDANT. One of the best mordants for zinc is known as the Dutch mordant, although many will find perchloride of iron very convenient, as it may be purchased solid and dissolved in water as required. Whichever is used, it will be wise to keep to the same and maintain the same strength as far as possible. The action of the mordant naturally depends on its strength and temperature, and it is only when these are constant that the process of etching can be regulated with any certainty.

The colder or weaker the mordant the longer it will take in its work. As its cost is not great and no large amount will be used, it would, therefore, be best to have fresh for each plate, but the temperature cannot be regulated so easily and, therefore, allowance must be made for this. In winter the work must be carried out in a warm room, and the dish, plate and bottle of mordant slightly warmed before etching, and greater accuracy will be obtained by the regular use of a thermometer.

Some etchers work very methodically with a thermometer, and a hydrometer specially constructed for their work, which shows the strength of the mordant. With these a table is drawn up showing the time to be allowed for various temperatures and strengths of acid. Some etch more or less by guess-work, judging by the amount of bubbling that takes place, and feeling the depth of the line with the point of the needle. Others etch a small scrap of metal at the same time as the plate, testing the lines on this scrap as they work. Another method is to have the plate a little larger than the picture is intended to be, and to needle portions of the margin. These portions may then be cleaned and tested by rubbing ink in them as the work progresses, and the whole of the spare margin cut off when the work is finished.

MAKING A TEST PLATE. Still another plan is to prepare a plate like Plate 22, and to etch it in sections. Needle the whole plate and place it in the bath. When it has etched for five minutes stop out one section and give the remainder another five minutes. Then stop another section and continue thus, so that each section has double the period of the previous one. A print from this plate will then serve as a working guide.

When the plate is placed in the bath and well covered with mordant the etching proper commences as soon as bubbles form on the lines. These are caused by the dissolving metal and must be wiped away gently with a feather. This will enable the process to be watched, and also prevent uneven etching.

The lightest lines of the picture will only require a short period of etching. When they are considered deep enough the plate is taken out of the bath, rinsed thoroughly, and dried on blotting paper. The parts that will require no further biting are then covered over with stopping varnish. This is an acid-resisting liquid that will dry quickly. It may be bought or prepared. Shellac varnish will serve excellently. It is applied with a fine brush, and it must not be so thin as to run over the plate, or creep up any lines that are not required to be covered.

After this first stopping out the plate is replaced in

the bath until the next depth of line is attained, when the washing, drying, and stopping out are repeated.

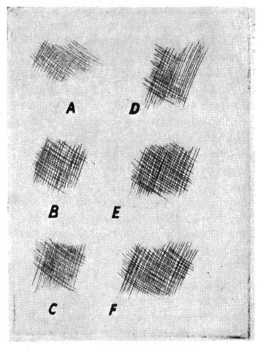

PLATE 22

ETCHING: A TEST PLATE

(Mordant, perchloride of iron)
A. Etched for ten minutes.
B. Etched for twenty minutes; and so on.

Thus the work is continued until finished, when the plate is finally washed and cleaned. A careful watch should be kept during the etching for any bad biting. Pinholes may start where the ground has not properly covered the plate, portions of the ground may chip off in unexpected places, or the edges may bubble badly. In any such case the plate must be removed, washed, dried and stopped in the usual way before the damage has become appreciable.

CLEANING THE PLATE. To clean the plate it is only

PLATE 23

MAN WITH SPADE   *Callot*

necessary to wipe it with a rag dipped in some solvent suited to the materials previously used. Thus, shellac varnish stopping will require methylated spirit; the usual ground will need turpentine: while a home-made ground will require the liquid with which it was prepared. Wipe the plate thoroughly clean—front, back and edges—and if the latter were not bevelled and polished in the first instance this is the time to do it.

A Trial Proof. Perhaps, the most exciting moment of all has now arrived, for a proof of the plate is to be taken, and the effect of all the previous work tested. The process of printing is gone into in the next chapter, so we will assume that the reader takes his first proof and compares it with the original drawing. The following are the most likely troubles, and in their remedy much care must be taken or the plate will be worsened instead of bettered by the treatment.

Scratches and other Unwanted Marks. To erase these a burnisher is required. It consists of a hard steel spindle with a round blunt point. The metal is rubbed with this (with a drop of oil) so that it is pressed down and polished until the scratch or pinhole is burnished away. If too deep for this to be done the metal is scraped with a triangular instrument that has sharp edges. Scrape gently in one direction, taking care that the point of the scraper does not itself make a scratch until the metal is again smooth, and then polish the part with a burnisher.

If much scraping has been done the plate will be hollow in that part and will have to be carefully wiped after the inking. For good work the plate should be hammered from the back (on a small anvil) until such hollows are brought up to the level of the rest of the plate; but it is hardly necessary for the beginner to tackle such work.

Underbitten Lines. Where parts of the picture do not print heavily enough, and it is ascertained that this is not due to bad inking or printing, they must be rebitten. This is a rather delicate experiment in which the plate is regrounded without filling the lines. In order to do this the plate must first be thoroughly cleaned. The ink left from the proof must be got out of all the lines that are to be re-etched—the others do not matter. This is best done by brushing with a small hoghair brush and turpentine. Then the plate must be warmed and gone over with the dabber which is grounded from another plate that has a warm ground on it. Very little of the ground must be used, and it must not be rubbed on the etched plate, but gently dabbed on it so that it is very evenly and thinly covered while the lines remain clear. Then the parts which want no re-etching are stopped out, the back and edges painted, and the plate placed in the bath.

Watch it very carefully for the ground may be so thin in some parts that unwanted biting may commence. If so, the plate must be immediately removed and treated in the usual way—wash, dry and stop. If only small sections want rebiting this may be done without repainting the edges and back. When the surface is grounded take a drop of strong hydrochloric acid on the end of the feather and wipe it on the spot to be etched deeper. As the action of the acid will be vigorous, only a few seconds of such treatment will be necessary, after which the plate must be well washed.

It is, perhaps, hardly necessary to say that while etching plenty of water should be handy. If not done near a water-tap, a pail of water by the side will be quite suitable in which to swill a small plate in order to stop all action of the mordant.

OTHER METHODS. The above is a general outline of etching, but there are obviously many variants, and each etcher has his own method of work, and often devises some fresh detail in the process. Thus, Seymour Haden needled the plate in the bath; the darkest lines

FIRST PROOF

PLATE 24

SECOND PROOF

The first proof shows underbitten lines.
The second proof is from the same plate after it had been regrounded
and rebitten.

being done first, and while they were etching, proceeding to the next ones, and so on, thus getting a very large gradient of tone.

A more simple method, and one that obviates stopping out, is to needle and etch the plate in sections.

PLATE 25

The whole plate needled and bitten for ten minutes; then sky stopped out and the rest bitten for a further twenty minutes. Dutch mordant.

This is only applicable in certain cases, and the etcher will, of course, vary his method according to the nature of the subject. Thus, a scene with clearly-defined foreground and distance may be done in stages. The foreground may be needled and etched; then the distance needled, and while this is being etched, the foreground is biting for a further period. This requires

some judgment in order to allow for the second period
of biting of the foreground, but it is, after all, only
another form of the stopping-out process.

PLATE 26

BRIDGE   *J. Greeno* (age 13)

Foreground needled, etched, and then stopped out. Distance then put
in with a fine needle and bitten for a short time. Perchloride bath.

A reverse method may be practised—etching the sky
and distance only and then stopping it out, and then
working on the foreground as if on a new plate. Some
simple subjects may only need a single biting; or if
there is a clear horizon, the plate may be tilted in the

bath so that the landscape only is immersed and bitten, and then the plate wholly immersed for a short final biting, in which the sky will be etched.

Thus there is plenty of scope for ingenuity, for these and other methods that may occur to the etcher may be tried singly or combined. It would certainly be best to start with some simple subject that only requires one biting. Thus, Plate 24, was a first experiment in etching, and, as may be seen, the needle was used too much like a pencil, and where thin lines were wanted not enough pressure was used to remove the ground properly. A thin greasy film was left that retarded the biting in those places. After the first proof the plate was, therefore, cleaned and very lightly regrounded; a few fresh lines (which had not come out at all in the proof) were needled; and the plate bitten for a short time. The result is shown in Plate 24 (second state).

As a second experiment some such subject as Plate 25 should be tried. All the lines were needled, and after ten minutes in the mordant the plate was removed and the sky stopped out. A further twenty minutes etching was then given to the foreground.

With Plate 26, the other method was adopted. Only the bridge and foreground were needled, and then etched for half an hour. The plate was then taken out, washed, dried, and the distance needled and immersed in the mordant for another ten minutes. This obviated the stopping-out process which would have necessitated some careful work under the arches of the bridge.

AQUATINT

Another interesting form of etching is known as aquatint from the fact that it somewhat resembles a

PLATE 27

FISHING BOAT ARRIVED   *E. W. Cooke*

Original size: there are twenty people clearly visible in the boats!

water-colour drawing. For this process a special ground
is used, so that if the plain-grounded plate were etched
in the acid bath and then cleaned, it would print as an
evenly-tinted rectangle, the depth of the colour depending on the length of time the plate had been in
the bath. It will thus be seen that one has only to etch
various parts of the plate for differing periods to obtain
a picture of graded tones.

DUST GROUND. The aquatint ground may be laid in
liquid form or as a dust. The former is a very trouble-
some process, but the latter may be done in various
ways. The usual method is to use a dust box. This
may consist of a box with a door to it, mounted so that
it can be revolved rapidly. Finely-powdered resin is
placed in this, the door shut and the box turned several
times until the interior is full of the dust. The door is
then opened, the plate placed in it face upwards on a
little shelf, and shut in for a few minutes until the dust
has settled on it.

Another method of filling the interior of the box with
dust is to stand it on the table and insert the nozzle
of a hand-bellows in a small hole near the base and
vigorously blow the resin dust which has been placed
inside. The plate is then inserted as with the previous
method. It must be removed without any jerk or
draught, or the even layer of dust will be disturbed,
and placed on the hot plate where the specks of resin
will melt and adhere to the surface, leaving minute
interstices which will be open to the attack of the
mordant.

An even more simple way of laying the ground is
to place the plate in the bottom of a box with an open
top and side. Stretch two or three pieces of fine muslin

PLATE 28

YARMOUTH HERRING BOAT (LUGGER)   *E. W. Cooke*
UNLOADING AT THE QUAY

across the top and then sprinkle resin powder so that it falls through the muslin as through a sieve, covering the plate evenly with dust. Avoid draughts, and when the plate looks properly covered remove it to the hot plate.

The specks of resin, of course, resist the acid, so that if the plate were now bitten it would be uniformly covered with microscopic pits which would hold the ink.

SAND GROUND is another method of obtaining the same result. For this the plate is covered in the usual way with ordinary ground. It is then put on the bed of the press, a piece of sand-paper laid on it, and run through the rollers with moderate pressure. This is done three or four times, shifting the sand-paper each time, so that the grains of sand crush through the ground and leave specks of the plate bare all over the surface as evenly as possible.

By any of these methods we thus get a plate on which the ground is broken up by innumerable pin-holes, and the best way of testing the effect is to prepare a small plate thus, and etch it in sections. Plate 29 shows such a plate bitten in the Dutch bath in equal sections. The whole was immersed for five minutes and then the top fifth stopped out. After another five minutes the next fifth was stopped, and so on.

This will serve as a guide in making a proper aquatint. For that, first prepare the sketch on paper in washes of water-colour black ; making it with various depths of colour—white, grey, pale black, dark black, as required. Then on the plate stop out those parts which are to be white, and bite the plate for a short

PLATE 29

AQUATINT

A test plate prepared with ordinary ground and sand paper. Bitten in five minute sections.

time. Then wash and dry it, and stop out the lighest
tint and re-bite. Then stop out the next darker section,
continuing thus until the whole plate has been bitten
variously according to the number of tints in the working drawing.

Aquatints are generally printed with coloured inks.
Some, such as Nocturnes, may be done in monochrome,
the whole plate being inked with a suitable colour, and
wiped and printed in the usual way. Others may be
done in two or more colours, in which case care must
be taken that the inks are kept within their proper
limits.

If lines are used in an aquatint they may be etched,
drypoint, or softground, but in any case they must not
be too bold or they will clash with the even tints of
the rest of the plate. In Plate 30 the outlines are soft-
grounded, and a fine dust ground was laid for the
distant sky and mountains, while a coarse ground was
used for the foreground.

Soft Ground Etching.

Soft ground etching is an interesting form of the art
in which the effect of a pencil-drawing is attained. It
is in fact done with the pencil instead of the needle, and
is thus especially attractive for those who prefer that
medium either for use or effect.

The work is done, as its name indicates, with a soft
ground, which is composed of about equal parts of the
ordinary dark ground and tallow. The drawing is done
on paper laid over the prepared plate, and when this
paper is pressed by the pencil it takes up the ground
and leaves the bare metal free to be etched. Thus, it is
important to see that the ground is properly prepared,

PLATE 30

for if too hard it will not adhere to the back of the
drawing-paper, and if too soft it is liable to come away
from the plate when not desired. It may be purchased
ready for use, but if mixed as required the proportions

PLATE 31

TREES: A SOFT GROUND ETCHING   E. Agass (age 13)

There is some foul biting at the tops of the trees. There was also some
in the sky, which was cleared with scraper and burnisher.

may be adjusted to suit the temperature—a little more
tallow in cold weather and a little less in hot weather.

LAYING THE GROUND. The surface of the plate must
be carefully cleansed from grease by wiping it with a
clean rag and turpentine and then with whitening
before it is grounded, and it must not be touched by the
fingers afterwards. The grounding is done in the usual
way, but a dabber reserved for this purpose must be

used and had better be specially marked so that it does not get confused with the hard ground dabber. The surface must not be touched after this process or the ground will be scratched or marked. It is imperative to see that the plate is thoroughly clean before grounding it, and that it is thoroughly covered by the ground. The latter has a nasty knack of collecting in minute hills if the plate is too hot, and of coming off in specks if too cold; in either case leaving pinholes of clear plate, which will etch. As soon as discovered they must be stopped out, but a lot of damage may be done before their discovery. Thus, in Plate 31, some foul biting may be seen, in spite of the care with which the work was done.

TRACING PAPER. The paper used must be a rather hard tissue, preferably slighly ribbed, as this gives a better pencil effect. It should be cut about an inch larger all round than the plate so that it may be stretched over the face and the edges gummed down on the back to prevent it slipping, Then the drawing is done with a hard pencil, using it in the normal manner, but taking care not to rest the hand or fingers on the paper.. It would be advisable first to make a tracing on the paper as the drawing must be carried out without any mistake. To do this prepare a drawing the size of the plate, place the tissue paper over it, mark round the edges and trace the chief outlines very lightly. Then place the tracing face downwards on the table, put the plate—ground downwards—on to it so that the edges coincide with the lines marked on the paper, and fold the edges over and fasten them down on the back of the plate with paste or gummed paper.

DRAWING. Now turn the plate over, and if there is

PLATE 32
A SOFT GROUND ETCHING
J. Rogers (age 13)

any difficulty in carrying out the drawing without touching its surface, make a hand-rest by placing the ends of a piece of board on two books. The drawing is to be done with a hard pencil used in the ordinary way and making thick and thin strokes, shading, etc., guided by the tracing and the original sketch. Be careful not to miss any parts, for it will be difficult to add to the work once the paper is removed. If it is desired to examine the work while it is being done, only two adjacent edges of the paper need be fixed, leaving a free corner that may be lifted up to examine the plate, when it will then be seen that the ground has attached itself to the paper and come away from the plate where lines have been made.

ETCHING. When finished, the plate is carefully stripped and the edges and back painted out, and then etched in the usual way. No stopping-out is necessary as the lines have already been varied in strength by the pencil work. They will be found rather uneven in texture owing to the ribbed paper which was used expressly for the purpose of giving this pencil or chalk line effect.

When the bubbling commences the feather will have to be used most lightly or it will scratch the ground, and it will be found safer merely to rock the dish as if developing a photographic plate in order to shift the bubbles.

When the biting is considered finished, remove the plate and examine it; and if the lines are deep enough wash and clean the plate and take a proof.

ALTERATIONS. The chief troubles to be met with will be either that the lines have not etched sufficiently in parts owing to the ground not having come away

THE TOMBSTONE

PLATE 33

A soft ground etching.

Gainsborough

cleanly, or that some of the ground has come away in patches and scratches and allowed unwanted etching. In the latter case the scraper and burnisher may be used effectively, but for the former trouble there is not much remedy.

The work is subject to accidents of various kinds, at least in the hands of the beginner, because of the soft nature of the ground which is so easily injured, and also because the proper working of the ground depends so largely on climate. A good deal of practice will probably be required before a good print is produced, but it will be found well worth the trouble for there is a great charm of quality about the soft ground etching that can be obtained in no other manner.

CHAPTER V

THERE is a special method of printing for each of the three forms mentioned at the beginning of this book. Relief-printing is done with a pressure vertical to the plate, lithography has to have a rubbing motion, and intaglio-printing is carried out by rollers. The latter, with which we are dealing, is necessary, because the paper has to be pressed heavily into the lines of the plate, and this is best done by the combined forward and downward movement which a roller gives.

THE PRESS. The copper-plate press (as it is called) is therefore very much like the homely mangle, the chief difference being that there is a travelling bed between the rollers. It is on this that the plate and paper are laid, and while the bed travels along on the under roller, the upper one presses the paper firmly into the lines of the plate. There is, as one would expect, a soft packing between roller and paper, and for this purpose a special blanketing is made. There are two sorts of blanket, a fine close one, called fronting, which goes on the paper, and a more springy one which goes next to the roller.

It will be necessary for the etcher to have a good press, and this will necessitate the only big outlay for the work. The presses of Rembrandt's time have not been essentially altered, although they are now made of steel throughout, and a geared handle takes the place of the "star," in the more expensive machines.

63

It is advisable to buy the best and biggest press that one can afford, for even small work is thus done much more satisfactorily; but a splendid little machine (Plate 34) with six-inch rollers is now available for two guineas—a sum considerably smaller than that entailed by many hobbies.

PAPER. Before commencing the printing it is necessary to prepare the paper. It should be cut to size,

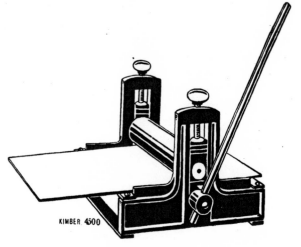

PLATE 34
A SMALL COPPER-PLATE PRESS

leaving a considerable margin round the plate, and then damped. If proof paper is used this may be done just before the printing, but more substantial paper for the finest proofs must be damped overnight. For this two boards, or sheets of zinc or glass, will be required. Two pieces of plate-glass are most convenient as they are perfectly flat, solid, and weighty. Have a nice, clean sponge and a bowl of water by the side, lay a sheet of paper on one piece of glass and go all over it with the damp sponge. Then turn it over and sponge the other side. The paper will then probably swell and wrinkle, so it is again reversed and sponged down *quite flat* on the other glass. Damp the next piece of paper in the same way and lay it squarely on the first sheet, and so do the batch of papers, placing one sheet of glass on top and pressing it down firmly. The papers should then form a solid mass without either bubble or crease, when they may be stood aside with a weight on the top glass. Next day they should be found soft and pliable, but without any visible moisture; and, of course, without a crease, for such would ruin the print.

INKING THE PLATE. The next process is to ink the plate. For this the jigger and heater will be required, as well as a dabber, some copper-plate ink, and an odd piece of glass or zinc on which to put a small portion of ink for immediate use.

The ink is of a very thick consistency, and had better be obtained ready for use. The etcher will suit his own taste as to whether it is black or brown, the general tone used being a warm black to avoid harshness in printing.

The plate, its face, back and edges thoroughly clean, is placed on the heater, and when quite warm (too hot to handle) is shifted to the jigger. The dabber is then inked from the inking plate and dabbed over the etching. It must be used firmly so that the ink is well pressed into the lines. Now warm the plate again, and when it is cool, wipe it.

WIPING THE PLATE. To do this two or three rags are necessary. The material used is a muslin netting

PLATE 35

Drypoint

J. Rogers (age 13)

Upper proof. Clean wiped.
Lower proof. Clean wiped only in parts.

made stiff with dressing. Make a pad of this, with no sharp edges or creases, and wipe the surface of the plate without using any pressure and being careful not to drag any ink out of the lines. When fairly clean take another piece of muslin formed into a pad and wipe the plate thoroughly as though polishing it. If the pad is quite smooth and moved with a firm circular motion it will drive what remains of the surface ink into the lines, giving a practically clean plate with well-filled lines. It is not necessary to make the plate perfectly clean as the whole surface of the print should have a slight even tint which is visible against the white paper which borders it.

Do not use any ordinary rag for the wiping as, if it is soft, it will pull the ink out of the lines. The proper stuff is very cheap and being stiff it does not drag the ink. Take about half a yard of it, crumple it up in the hands and then make a smooth pad of it. This may be used many times as it is, for although it will become covered with ink, it will still partially clean the plate, the lines thereon even drawing some of the ink from the pad itself. After a time another part of the muslin may be drawn over the surface of the pad, and the second pad used for the final polishing may be treated in the same way.

RETROUSAGE. A final wiping may be done with a soft muslin, this drawing some of the ink out of the lines on to the smooth plate. This is known as retrousage and softens the picture, but it must not be overdone. Plate 35 is an exaggerated example of this, the ink, especially on the walls of the barn, being spread between the lines. The retrousage muslin must be used lightly, and if only small parts want treating, a corner of the rag may be twisted up into a sort of stump, and the lines gently worked with it where necessary. Plate 36 shows a more normal use of this method,

PLATE 36

A COTTAGE (DRYPOINT)   *M. Lane (age* 11)

all the lines in this little sketch being softened by a final wiping of the retrousage rag.

It is, however, a process that may do more harm than good, and a nice clean proof is generally to be preferred. It is akin to the practice of leaving ink over the plate in patches to get a mezzotint effect, and is heartily condemned by many. However, there are no definite rules in art, and the best way for the beginner to proceed is to examine all the available etchings by the masters, and then work according to one's taste that has been formed by this study.

PREPARING THE PRESS. The press must now be adjusted for work. Take an uninked plate, place it at about the middle of the bed, cover it with a piece of blotting paper and the blankets, and pass it through the press. This will require considerable power, but the lever should be turned as gently and evenly as possible. When through, throw back the blankets and examine the blotting paper, which should show deeply the impression of the plate. If one side has not been so deeply marked as the other it shows that one adjusting screw should be turned a little lower. Do this and try again, so arranging these screws that the plate mark, as this impressed edge is called, is even throughout.

PRINTING. Now the inked plate may be printed. Warm it slightly and place it on the bed, on it place squarely one of the damped papers, on this lay a piece of fresh blotting paper, and then the blankets. Pass through the press, throw back the blanket, and lift the papers carefully from the plate. Separate the proof from the blotting paper, pulling them gently apart.

If it is a good proof all the lines will have come out clearly, and on examining the back of the paper the lines will show as minute depressions where the paper has been forced into the lines of the plate.

These are the more common faults—

Spotty patches of white. These are caused by specks of moisture on the paper. Examine each sheet before placing it on the plate, and if there is any sign of water dab it off with a piece of blotting paper.

White lines. These may be due to lack of ink, but

more probably to insufficient pressure. As stated above, an examination of the back of the paper will show whether it has been pressed right into the lines.

Grey lines show that the ink was not pressed sufficiently into them, or that it was afterwards pulled out in cleaning the plate.

Streaks or smudges of ink are due to insufficient cleaning of the surface.

Dirty edges will be found if the plate has not had its edges bevelled and burnished, and care must be taken to wipe these after the final polishing in the inking process, as some ink will probably have been left on them.

Cut edges are due, not to too much pressure, but to insufficient bevelling of the plate.

There is, of course, an art in printing which has to be learned by experience, but attention to the above details will help one far on the road to success.

BLOTTING PAPER. When printing, a fresh piece of blotting paper must be used for each proof, for a used piece will show the plate mark and will give an uneven pressure at that part if used again. These used pieces will, however, serve for other purposes, such as taking up any moisture that may be on the proof papers, for drying the prints, and for placing under the dish and bottle of mordant to mop up stray drips. Destroy all paper used for the latter purpose.

The blankets should be watched, and not always used in exactly the same position, and when they begin to get hard they may be washed carefully in warm water. They must be kept dry while in use.

PROOF PAPERS. There are many varieties of paper made for etching, and it would be most advisable for the reader to obtain a sample packet and decide for himself which sort he prefers, both for work and effect.

The tone of the paper should be chosen according to the plate which is being printed. White does not suit all styles and a pale amber or coffee tint is preferred by many, partly, perhaps, because it has a suggestion of antiquity. However, such a tinge does give a warmth and depth to many pictures and should be used for this purpose. On the other hand, a bluish or greenish tone will enhance the printing from some plates.

VARIOUS INKS. The colour of the ink should also be considered in reference to the plate and the paper used, and while black will be the main colour, it may have added to it any of the usual reds and browns, yellows or blues for warm or cold effects. These colours may, of course, be used by themselves, but, except for the browns, they should not be unless for some very special purpose.

AFTER TREATMENT OF PROOFS. By the intaglio process of printing the thickness of ink on the paper is quite appreciable, and this characteristic should not be destroyed by pressing the proofs immediately after printing. The proof as it comes damp from the press has a charm which is the delight of the printer. The paper is perfectly flat, except for the delicate ridges of ink on the ridges of paper, the latter caused by the impression into the etched lines and seen as grooves on the back of the print.

Unfortunately, some of this pristine beauty is gone when the paper becomes crinkled and buckled as it dries. To avoid this without spoiling the proofs is the difficulty. As they are taken from the press they may be laid between sheets of blotting paper and a very slight weight placed upon them when a small pile has been formed, but if too much pressure is put on them too soon some of the ink will be removed.

If perfect flatness is required the proofs must be damped again (sponging will not injure them once the ink is dry) and interleaved with blotting paper and put

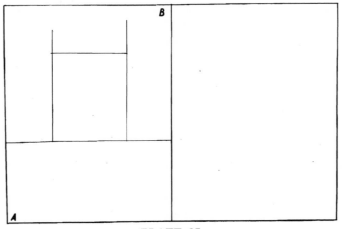

PLATE 37

under heavy pressure, changing the blotting paper for fresh dry pieces in an hour or two's time and renewing the pressure. This will, of course, largely destroy the raised surface of the paper at the lines and the plate mark. For any special proof the best way is to paste its edges down on a drawing-board or fix them with gummed strips while still damp from the press—just as a paper is stretched for a water-colour drawing— and then cut round the outside of the plate mark when the paper is dry and taut.

If the picture is to be framed its edges may be

pasted to the under side of a stiff mounting-board in which a suitable aperture has been cut, and left to dry under pressure, but this would only be suitable for small prints as large ones would buckle the mount in drying. To cut such a mount should not be difficult with a sharp knife and bevelled rule (preferably iron).

MOUNTING. A good way of keeping proofs is to mount each in a sheet of stiff paper, doubled like a sheet of note-paper, and with an opening cut through the top page to suit the style of the picture. Allow plenty of margin to the mount which should be widest at the bottom. Thus, for the general size of plate recommended in a previous chapter a sheet of paper (good white drawing paper will do) about 19×12 inches would be a suitable size. This is folded down the middle and the opening marked on AB, Plate 37, a little larger than the print—allowing the plate mark to show. If the latter is $4\frac{1}{2} \times 3$ inches the opening should be about an eighth of an inch bigger at top and sides, and a quarter of an inch at the bottom. Then with rule and square lightly draw the outline as in the illustration and cut the opening. A sheet of glass is the best thing to use for a cutting board, although it blunts the knife rather quickly : keep the tool sharp or it will tear the paper.

The flattened proof is then gummed at the two top corners and placed face downwards over the opening so that when the mounting paper is folded over it appears as Plate 38, the title and artist's name appearing between the bottom edge of the mount and the plate mark.

Proofs which are wider than they are high will naturally require mounting the other way, and each mount

PLATE 38

must be cut to suit the individual picture. Thus, a drawing with heavy foreground should be fairly high up in the mount, while one with the heaviest lines near the top can be placed in a more central position.

Some pictures may demand a different sized mount, but it will be most convenient to keep to a standard size if possible, as the collection is thus much easier to handle in a portfolio.

CHAPTER VI

HOME-MADE APPARATUS AND MATERIALS

PLATES. For practice work, thick zinc sheeting may be purchased from a good builders' warehouse and cut to size. No. 20 W.G. will be suitable, provided it is rolled quite flat before purchase. It may be cut with a strong knife by scoring it through from both sides until it will snap in the fingers ; but a fine metal saw, will probably be found more convenient to handle.

The edges must be filed smooth, and the best side for the working surface chosen and slightly bevelled at the edges, so that they will not cut either paper or blankets when in the press. This surface and bevel must then be highly polished—a rather tedious job. Rub first with fine emery-cloth and then with an oil rag dipped in the finest emery-flour. A vigorous rubbing with a good knife-powder should follow this, and then a final polish with plate-powder. Thoroughly clean the plate between each process so that no coarse material is carried into a finer polishing powder, or the whole aim of the work—which is to produce a mirror like surface without a scratch—will be frustrated. If the surface is in good condition when purchased, a vigorous rubbing with metal-polish will suffice.

GROUND. These generally consist of wax, gum and asphaltum or bitumen. Several receipts are given in the Appendix. To mix such a one as Bosse's ground the following amounts of each material should be purchased.

Bees-wax	.	.	.	.	. 1 oz.
Gum Mastic		.	.	.	. 10 dr.
Bitumen Powder	.		.	.	. 5 dr.

First, melt the wax in a double container—a small jar in a saucepan of water will serve. Then add the gum, stirring meanwhile with a glass rod, and when this is melted, sprinkle in the Bitumen. Continue stirring and let simmer for about ten minutes and then turn it into a pail of cold water. After well wetting the hands work the ground (which will be like a black putty) into a ball, squeezing out all the water. When hard, keep in a dustproof box.

A liquid ground may be prepared by dissolving a black stove enamel in petrol and dipping the plate in a bath of it, but no doubt many enamels will dry brittle, and chip in the needling, so that a little experiment may be necessary in order to find a suitable material. The solution should be quite thin, when it will cover the plate with a beautiful light-brown film.

PLATE 39

A DABBER

Dip the plate into the bath (a photographer's dish) face downwards so that any sediment which may be in the liquid will be on the back, and the plate should then be leaned against a box (or some such object) with its face on the underside so that no dust will settle on it. It should be used as soon as it is dry enough to handle.

A DABBER. Cut a disc of cardboard about one and a half inches in diameter. Lay a square of silk or kid out flat; on it place a wad of soft rag, and on top place the card disc and then a bit more rag. Gather up the edges of the square and bind them together tightly

about the card so that a firm pad is made. It must be
kept in a box so that no foreign matter will collect on
its surface. After its first use it should be warmed for
subsequent dabbings, in order to soften the ground on
its surface.

An ink dabber may be made in the same way but it
should be firmer and its covering more solid. A piece of
chamois leather will do, but printers often use a piece of
old stocking. When not in use its face should rest in
linseed-oil, which will prevent the ink on its surface
becoming hard. The superfluous oil must be removed
before using the dabber.

A HOT PLATE. A piece of thick sheet iron (14 W.G.)
ten inches by eight may be purchased, and holes drilled
at the corners and countersunk. Then cut four pieces
of iron rod, slightly larger in diameter than these holes,
for the legs, to the length required by the burner to be
used. File one end of each small enough to slip through
the holes in the plate, making a square shoulder on
which the plate will rest. Insert the legs and hammer
down the slight projection into the counter-sunk side,
so as to form a rigid little table, which will be most
stable if the legs are bent at the lower ends.   Plate 40
will make this clear.

A JIGGER. Measure the height of the hot plate, and
make a four-sided box, so that when it rests on one side
it will present a surface ten by eight, of exactly the
same height. It need only be glued and nailed, and if
a back is also nailed on it will be absolutely firm.

NEEDLES. If a thick sewing or darning needle is used
it may easily be inserted in a handle of any kind most
suitable to the individual. A dab of sealing-wax on
the junction of needle and holder will keep the former

secure in place. A gramophone needle may be used in place of the lead in a propelling pencil; or a fine steel knitting needle may be inserted in a piece of cork of convenient shape. In this latter case the needle must be sharpened and kept sharp, on an oilstone. This is done by placing the end of the needle nearly flat on the stone and holding it in the palm of the hand so that

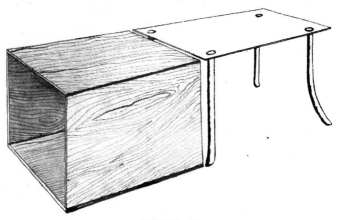

PLATE 40
JIGGER AND HOT PLATES

a revolving motion may be given to it as it is pressed downwards.

MORDANTS. If the solid mordant is purchased it only requires the addition of water, one pound being dissolved in about a pint and a quarter of the liquid. This, or any other mordant, is best kept in a glass-stoppered bottle and should be stored in a safe place.

To make Dutch mordant, if only a small quantity is required, it will suffice to obtain three drams of Potassium Chlorate from a chemist, and dissolve it in nine ounces of water, measured in a photographer's measuring glass. If the water is warm the crystals will dissolve more readily. Then add one ounce of pure hydrochloric acid, and pour the mixture into a glass-stoppered bottle by means of a glass funnel.

STOPPING AND VARNISH. One of the chief considerations in choosing a stopping out varnish is that it should dry quickly, for one does not want to wait an hour or two between each biting of the plate. It must also be sufficiently thick to allow of very accurate placing. It is often necessary to stop out patches just against a line that requires further etching, and the varnish, while coming freely from the brush, must not run or creep and so spoil the work.

Shellac varnish dries very quickly, and being of a different nature from the ground does not upset it in any way, as one of a kindred material may do. It is easily prepared by dissolving shellac in methylated spirit, and the latter must be used to clean it off when the biting is completed.

Put shellac into a small bottle (such as a medicine bottle) until it is about quarter full. Cover this with methylated spirit and leave it for a day or two, shaking occasionally. Insert a fine-pointed camel-hair brush through the cork (a rubber one is best) so that the hair is in the liquid. It will then always be ready for use. Try the varnish to see whether it allows of accurate use. If too thin, add more shellac; if too thick, add a very small quantity of spirit. When on the plate it will dry in a very few minutes.

A BURNISHER, such as in Plate 41, may be made by taking a hard steel rod and bending up one end of it. The end must be made red-hot in a Bunsen burner and then bent in the vice, and then hardened by dipping into water while hot. The other end should be well rounded on an emery-wheel and the whole thoroughly polished with emery-paper. To ensure a perfectly smooth surface on the parts which will be used to burnish the plate, a polisher may be made thus. Get a piece of hard wood and cut a rounded groove in it of the same diameter as the steel rod. Oil the groove

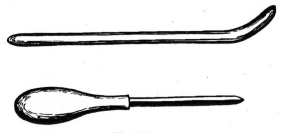

PLATE 41
BURNISHER AND SCRAPER

and sprinkle it with fine emery-powder, and then rub the rounded end and the knuckle of the burnisher up and down in this until its surface is perfect.

A SCRAPER may be made from an old triangular file. With an emery or carborundum wheel take off the teeth of the top half of the file and round the point (as in Plate 41) taking care to keep a very sharp edge at each of the three angles. Do not let the file get too hot while grinding it or its temper will be lost.

It is used, when scraping the plate, in one direction only—that is, towards the operator. If not perfectly sharp it will jump and jag the surface of the plate, but a keen edge will scrape off clean shavings. It should be kept sharp on an oilstone.

THE PRINTING PRESS. Rough proofs may be obtained with an ordinary mangle or wringer if the plate is laid on a smooth board, covered with plenty of packing and run through, but not enough pressure can really be obtained owing to the springs, which "give" too much.

The ingenious reader may, perhaps, alter a small mangle in order to overcome this difficulty, or may adapt some other piece of machinery. For instance, the boys, whose illustrations are included in this book, use a photographer's burnisher, which was obtained secondhand for a few shillings. It consists of an iron frame with two steel rollers, seven inches long and about an inch and a half in diameter, turned by a handle. A zinc plate is used for the "bed," and the blankets consist of from twenty to thirty sheets of rough paper—the pages of a cheap magazine. Smooth paper will not do as it is apt to slide, but the thick porous kind, like blotting paper, works admirably. It can easily be renewed, and the number of sheets is altered to suit various thicknesses of plate, which is a more simple matter than altering the adjusting screws of the top roller.

In fact, in any copper-plate press, it is bad policy to interfere with these screws once they are nicely adjusted. It takes some time to get them correct so that the pressure is perfectly even, and it will be found much more convenient to add an extra piece of blotting paper above the plate to get a greater pressure, than to move these screws.

For printing the compressed fibre drypoints, which do not require so great a pressure as etchings, a wooden press, such as that shown in Plate 42, may be constructed at small cost. If the reader has no lathe he may get the rollers made fairly cheaply by a professional turner, or, perhaps, by some friend. The rest of the job is straightforward and simple, but it must be done very

PLATE 42
A HOME-MADE PRESS

accurately in order to get strength and precision when printing.

The rollers are six inches long and two inches in diameter, and must be of well-seasoned wood, firmly fixed on iron spindles, which are mild steel rods three-eighths of an inch in diameter, the bottom one being seven inches and the upper one nine and a half inches long. Do not polish them, but if they are smooth, roughen them and then drive them into the wood for the rollers, which should have holes bored through them of slightly smaller diameter than the spindles— but not too small, or the wood will split. The top roller especially, must be incorporated with its spindle in some way so that it cannot work loose. This may be done by covering the iron with a little paste, made of sal-ammoniac and water, as it is forced through the wood.

Use square pieces of wood for the rollers, of sufficient size to allow for any inaccuracy in boring, and then rough them up and turn to two inches in the lathe. If possible, turn the ends of the spindles also, otherwise they must be polished by hand. They will project half an inch each end of the bottom roller, and half an inch on one side of the top roller, and three inches on the other. This long part must be squared at the end to take the handle.

The bearings of the rollers consist of two iron plates screwed to the sides of the press, as is clearly shown in the photograph. To make these, get two pieces of soft iron, one eighth of an inch thick, one and three-quarter inches wide, and six inches long. Place them face to face in a vice and drill the hole, A, as in Plate 43. Now fasten them together by means of a small bolt and nut through the hole. Then drill B and bolt together, and this will enable you to get the holes for the spindle dead accurate. The lower one must be one and three-quarter inches from the bottom, and the higher one two and a half inches above it, and just large enough for the rollers to turn easily. Also drill the other four holes for the screws; take the plates apart and countersink the screw-holes on the faces that were together when bolted. Now with the six-inch roller, the one-eighth plates and two one-eighth washers, the distance between the sides of the press will be six and a half inches, and the framework must be made accordingly.

Use well-seasoned hard wood, one inch thick, and cut the base twelve by six and a half; the sides twelve by seven, cutting off the top corners, as shown, allowing about two inches in the middle on which to fix the top cross-bar. Then screw the side-pieces to the sides of the base. Greater rigidity will be obtained if they are rabbeted, as shown in the illustration, in which case the base will have to be half an inch wider than as given above. But this is not absolutely necessary.

The next parts to prepare are the four pieces to carry the bed. These consist of inch wood, four and three-quarter inches long and two and three-quarter inches wide. Round the ends, as shown in the photograph, and then take a few shavings off the top so that they will not be quite as high as the top of the lower roller. They will thus support either ends of the bed without retarding its movement through the rollers. Place them in position, a quarter of an inch from each side of the roller, and screw them to the sides and also to the

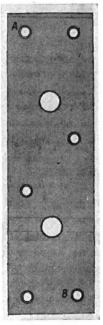

PLATE 43
BEARING PLATE
FOR PRESS

bottom so that they also serve as angle blocks for rigidity.

Next cut the top bar with half laps, the distance between these being exactly six and a quarter inches—the length of the rollers, plus the two one-eighth washers. It will then fit tightly between the tops of the iron bearing plates.

Now mark the positions of the iron plates, and taking the woodwork to pieces, screw them on exactly level with the base, and exactly at right angles to it. Insert the spindles in position and screw the whole frame up firmly, when the rollers should be exactly parallel and square with the sides, and easily turned without any looseness.

The projecting spindle, which has been squared may carry any sort of handle. The one in the illustration consists of two wooden bars joined with a half lap and firmly secured by a square iron plate screwed on each side to each of the four arms. A square hole is cut through the wood and iron to fit on the spindle which is threaded at the end to take a wing nut. If this cannot be done a flat piece of wood or iron may be pierced to fit the spindle and held in position by a split pin passed through a hole in the spindle, or merely driven on tightly.

The construction may, of course, be varied in any way to suit the convenience of the individual; the only two essentials being that the rollers must be parallel, as any means of varied regulation would be beyond the scope of the average reader; and that they must be square with the sides, or the bed will be driven askew and thus jam.

For the bed all that is required is a piece of wood six inches by twelve, and about three-eighths inch thick.

It must be perfectly flat and of even thickness. The thinner this wood the more blanketing will be required, and it would be a good plan to cover this bed with a sheet of zinc, and to try two or three thicknesses of wood in order to see which is best for printing. Too much blanketing will be awkward to work, while if there is not enough the paper will not be forced into the lines of the plate.

This, or any other press, must be screwed down firmly to a heavy solid table, for the turning of the roller necessitates enough force to move a light bench all over the room.

A LIGHT SCREEN will be found very useful when working on the plate. It may be made from ground glass, or tissue or tracing paper, and its object is to diffuse and soften the light so that the shining surface of the zinc will appear just like a white drawing paper.

If tracing paper is used, mount it on a light wooden frame about two feet square. Hinge this to the front or side edge of a drawing board and make a strut to support it at a convenient angle. The best position will easily be found by a little experiment.

If the working-bench is next to a window a frame may be made to rest on the window-ledge and hang forward on the slant, being kept in position by a piece of string fastened to the window-frame and the top of the screen by drawing-pins.

PRESERVING PLATES. The surface of a zinc plate will soon tarnish if left unprotected, so that if it is required to preserve any etched plate for future printing, its surface must be covered, and regrounding the plate is the simplest means of doing this. The plate is easily cleaned when necessary.

APPENDIX

RECIPES
GROUNDS

Bosse's for Dutch Mordant—

Bees-wax	5 parts by weight
Gum mastic . . .	3 ,, ,, ,,
Bitumen (powder) . .	1½ ,, ,, ,,

Rembrandt's—

White wax	30 parts by weight
Gum mastic . . .	15 ,, ,, ,,
Asphaltum . . .	15 ,, ,, ,,

Sir Frank Short's—

Bees-wax	5 parts by weight
Syrian asphaltum . .	4 ,, ,, ,,
Burgundy pitch . .	1 part ,, ,,
Black pitch . . .	1 ,, ,, ,,

Soft Ground—

One of the above mixed with an equal weight of tallow.

Transparent—

White wax	5 parts
Gum mastic	3 ,,

MORDANTS (FOR ZINC)

Dutch—

Hydrochloric acid	10 parts
Potassium chloride . . .	2 ,,
Water	88 ,,

Haden's—

Nitric acid	25 parts
Water	75 ,,
Or a weaker bath of nitric acid .	1 part
Water	7 parts

ABBREVIATIONS, Etc.

Delineator, del.	. . .	Draughtsman
Pinxit	. . .	Painter
Sculptor, sculpsit, sc.		
Incidit, inc.	} . .	Engraver
Eng. . .		
Imprimit, imp.	. . .	Printer
Excudit, exud.	. . .	Publisher (or Engraver)
Fecit, fec., f.	. . .	Etcher

Remarque. The thumb-nail sketch on the margins of etchings of the last century.

State. A proof from each stage of the etching is termed a state. The first state is thus a proof from the plate before any alterations or additions have been made. Subsequent states may, therefore, differ considerably from this.

Signed Proof. Having printed an edition, the artist selects all the best proofs and signs them just below the plate mark.

MATERIALS REQUIRED (with Approximate Cost)

Drypoint—

Compressed fibre sheets	. .	1s. 6d. per doz.
Knife: tool	. . . .	6d. each.
,, blades	. . . .	2d. each
Printer's ink	. . . .	1s. quarter lb.

Etching—

Zinc plates	. . . .	3s. to 4s. per sq. ft.
File, triangular		
Emery-paper, No. 000	. .	2d. per sheet
Oil		
Oilstone		
Ground	. . . . .	ball, 1s. 3d.
		liquid, 2s. per bottle
		soft, 1s. 3d. per ball
Dabber		
Needles: darning, gramophone, etc.		
Mordant, materials for mixing	.	A few pence
,, solid	. . .	1s. per lb.
Funnel, glass		
Feathers		

Dish, photographers' .	.	.	from 1s.
Measuring glass .	.	.	„ 9d.
Stopping-out varnish .	.	.	6d. per bottle
Burnisher . .	.	.	from 1s. 6d.
Scraper .	.	.	„ 3s.
Jigger .	.	.	„ 8s.
Hot plate .	.	.	„ 18s. 6d.

Printing—

Copper-plate press	.	.	from £2
Blankets . .	.	.	2s. to 3s. per sq. ft.
Ink . . .	.	.	from 2s. per lb.
Dabber			
Paper, 30 in. × 22 in. .	.	.	„ 3s. per quire
Blotting paper .	.	.	„ 2s. 6d. per quire
Damping plates—two sheets of zinc or glass			
Wiping canvas .	.	.	6d. per yard

General—

Magnifying glass, a fairly strong one of any kind			
Tracing paper .	.	.	2d. a sheet
Transfer paper—red or white	.		3d. a sheet
Turpentine			
Sand-paper (for aquatint)			
Detail paper (for soft ground etching) .	.	.	2d. a sheet